DRAWING CHIBI FOOD

Learn How To Draw
Kawaii Onigiri, Adorable Dumplings, Yummy Donuts, and Other Cute and Tasty Dishes

Illustrations by TESSA CREATIVE ART

ULYSSES BOOKS
FOR YOUNG READERS

T0204899

Published by:
ULYSSES BOOKS FOR YOUNG READERS
an imprint of Ulysses Press
PO Box 3440
Berkeley, CA 94703
www.ulyssespress.com

ISBN: 978-1-64604-7-093
Library of Congress Control Number: 2024934563

Printed in the United States
10 9 8 7 6 5 4 3 2 1

Acquisitions editor: Kierra Sondereker
Project manager: Paulina Maurovich
Managing editor: Claire Chun
Editor: Renee Rutledge
Proofreader: Barbara Schultz
Front cover design and artwork: Tessa Creative Art
Layout: Winnie Liu

CONTENTS

ASIAN FOOD

ONIGIRI

Onigiri are Japanese rice balls made in fun shapes like circles or triangles, and wrapped in seaweed.

STEP 1 Draw a rice ball in the shape of a rounded triangle. Create rough uneven lines to portray the texture of rice.

STEP 2 Add a curved diagonal line in the bottom left corner of the triangle.

Sketch a few more!

STEP 3

Create another curved diagonal line in the bottom right corner of the triangle. Erase where the two lines overlap. Draw two circle eyes, two smaller oval blush spots, and a rounded-*W* mouth.

STEP 4

Color in the bottom corners to depict seaweed. Make the eyes black with a few white spots. Add light coloring and slight texture to make your onigiri extra cute!

Sketch a few more!

Sketch a few more!

Try a few from scratch.

TAMAGOYAKI

Not your typical omelet, tamagoyaki is made with thinly rolled egg. Re-create the layers with a simple swirl and put a smile on your own pillow of eggy goodness!

STEP 1
Draw a rectangle. Erase the top two corners and connect the lines to create a 6-sided shape.

STEP 2
Create a line that separates the 6-sided shape. It should roughly resemble a trapezoid above a rectangle.

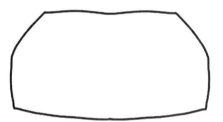

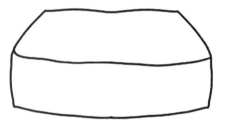

Sketch a few more!

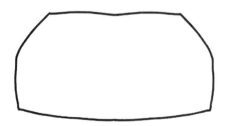

STEP 3

Draw a counterclockwise swirl pattern within the trapezoid to represent the top of the tamagoyaki and its famous rolled egg layers. Add two circle eyes, two small oval blush spots, and a tiny smile on the front of the tamagoyaki. Finish by drawing random splotches across the shape to add texture.

STEP 4

Darken the eyes and leave some white spots for highlights. Shade in your tamagoyaki, making the front slightly darker than the top.

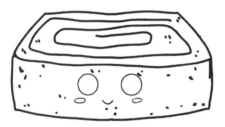 

Sketch a few more!

Try a few from scratch.

SUSHI

STEP 1

Sketch a long, somewhat lumpy, and curved oval. This is your thin slice of fish.

STEP 2

Underneath the oval, draw a cloud-like shape to make the rice. Add large black eyes with a few white spots. On top of your fish, draw a dollop of wasabi that looks a little like an upside-down heart.

Sketch a few more!

STEP 3

Erase the line covered by the wasabi. Draw a few squiggly lines on the fish and add a rounded *W*-shaped mouth between and a little below the eyes.

STEP 4

Finish bringing your sushi to life by shading the wasabi and fish. Then add some super-cute blush spots by the eyes.

Sketch a few more!

Try a few from scratch.

BENTO

The traditional Japanese lunch box is a trendy container for a meal on the go. With different compartments for sides and mains, lunch can be appetizing—and aesthetic.

STEP 1 To start your bento box, draw a rectangle at a slight angle. Add a line that runs from the top to the bottom of the rectangle. Make the rectangle 3D by drawing short vertical lines at the bottom-left, bottom-right, and top-right corners of the rectangle. Connect the lines and erase the vertical line at the bottom-right corner.

STEP 2 Add depth to your drawing by creating short and long horizontal lines across the front and the side of the bento box.

STEP 3 Start filling in your bento box with yummy ingredients! In the right compartment, add four ovals to represent meat. Draw repeating curved lines to represent noodles.

STEP 4

Add more repeating curved lines until the right compartment of your bento box is full.

STEP 5

In the left compartment, draw four pieces of nigiri sushi. Draw four lumpy oval shapes. On top of each lumpy oval, draw a different shape. On one, draw a rectangle, on another, draw a curved oval, on another draw, a fish, and on the last one, draw a lumpy parallelogram.

STEP 6

Fill in the rest of the left compartment by drawing five circular lumpy cloud shapes and two circles. Add some leafy green vegetables by drawing scalloped and curly lines from the top to the bottom of the left compartment. In the bottom of the right compartment, add a blob-shaped egg on top of the noodles.

STEP 7

On the front of the bento box, draw a face by adding two circle eyes, two small oval blush spots, and a tiny smile. Draw the same face on all four of the nigiri pieces. Add texture to the ingredients with squiggles, dots, and curved lines on the nigiri. Draw in the veins of the leafy green vegetables. Add an egg yolk by drawing a circle within the blob in the right compartment.

STEP 8

Finish by shading in your drawing! Darken the eyes and leave little white spots. Make the pieces of fish on top of the nigiri darker than the rice. Add swirls within the five circular lumpy cloud shapes to turn them into narutomaki (white fish cake).

Keep going from Step 1.

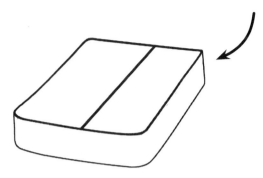

Try a few from scratch.

RAMEN

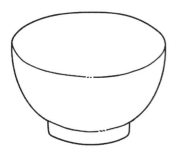

STEP 1

Draw a bowl by sketching an oval. Add a curved *U*-shaped line that connects to the oval above it. Create a foot for the bowl by drawing a short, thin rectangle underneath.

STEP 2

Add a rectangle coming out of the top-right side of the bowl to represent seaweed. Draw a couple of overlapping curved shapes in the bottom left of the bowl to add tonkatsu (Japanese pork cutlet) to your ramen.

STEP 3

Create ramen noodles by drawing repeating wavy lines within the bowl. Make sure to leave space between the wavy lines and the oval to create a rim for the bowl.

STEP 4

On the front of the bowl, sketch two circle eyes, two smaller oval blush spots, and a small smile. Add other ingredients to your ramen! Draw eggs by creating ovals with circles in them. Draw narutomaki by drawing cloud-like shapes with spirals within them. Add enoki mushrooms by drawing repeating thin rectangles with ovals on top. Add small rectangles for green onions. Don't forget to add chopsticks by drawing two thin rectangles at the top left of the bowl. Finish everything off by drawing short lines and dots to add depth and texture to the ingredients.

STEP 5

Shade in the different ramen ingredients. Color in the bowl and add a white stripe. Darken the eyes and leave white spots as highlights. Make sure to shade the sides of the bowl to create a 3D effect.

DRAWING CHIBI FOOD

Keep going from Step 1.

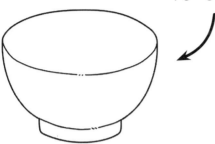

Try a few from scratch.

OMURICE

This fried rice omelet is often topped with ketchup—a favorite with kids!

STEP 1 Draw a lumpy oval that somewhat resembles a UFO.

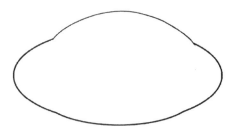

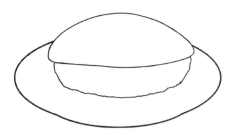

STEP 2 Using the top line of the UFO shape, draw a smaller lumpy oval with a flatter bottom to represent the omelet. Add a rough *U*-shaped curve underneath the flat bottom of the small lumpy oval to represent the rice.

STEP 3 Add texture to your omurice by drawing various squiggles and specks.

STEP 4 Draw a thick zig-zag line across the omelet.

STEP 5 Add two circle eyes, two smaller blush spots, and a tiny *U*-shaped smile. Sketch small jagged leaf shapes on both sides of the omurice.

STEP 6 Darken the eyes and leave small white spots for highlights. Shade in the omurice, making the leaves, omelet, and ketchup darker than the rice.

DRAWING CHIBI FOOD

Keep going from Step 1.

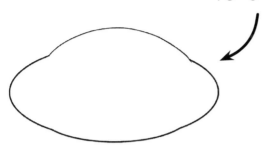

Try a few from scratch.

MISO SOUP

STEP 1
Start your bowl by drawing a rounded guitar pick shape. Create a foot for the bowl by drawing a short, thin rectangle underneath.

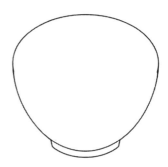

STEP 2
Within the rounded guitar pick shape, draw two concentric circles. Add short lines along the curves of the bowl to add depth.

STEP 3
Draw a curved line within the smaller circle to create the soup. Add seaweed to the miso soup by drawing large rectangular shapes.

STEP 4

On the front of the bowl, add two circle eyes, two smaller oval blush spots, and a rounded *W*-shaped mouth. Draw different miso soup ingredients. Add tofu by drawing cubes and triangles. Add some green onion by drawing small ovals with *C*-shaped lines within them.

STEP 5

Darken the eyes and leave white spots for highlights. Shade in your miso soup, making the rim and foot of the bowl, seaweed, and green onions darker than the soup. Add various curved white lines near the ingredients to help them look like they're floating.

ASIAN FOOD

DRAWING CHIBI FOOD

Keep going from Step 1.

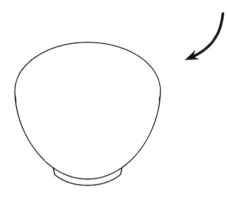

Try a few from scratch.

TONKATSU

 STEP 1 Draw an oval.

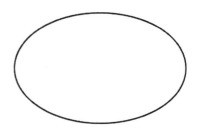

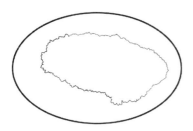

STEP 2 Within the oval, draw a random shape with jagged uneven edges to represent rice.

STEP 3 Add six overlapping cloud-like shapes to represent the tonkatsu. Draw various squiggles within the shapes to add depth.

STEP 4 Draw a smaller oval to create a rim for the plate. Add further texture to the rice by drawing more jagged lines.

STEP 5 In the bottom-right corner of the rice, draw two dark circle eyes with white spots for highlights, two small oval blush spots, and a rounded *W*-shaped mouth. Add small, dark, rounded shapes to represent green onions.

STEP 6 Erase any overlapping lines from the smaller oval. Shade in your drawing, making the plate and the tonkatsu darker than the rice.

Keep going from Step 1.

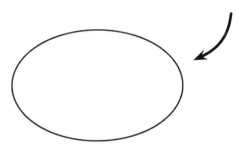

Try a few from scratch.

DUMPLINGS

STEP 1   Draw a wide *U*-shape.

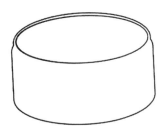

STEP 2   Draw an oval above the wide *U*-shape. Connect the top of the *U*-shape by going around the top of the oval to create the wooden steamer basket.

STEP 3   Add two dumplings by drawing rounded, slightly lumpy shapes.

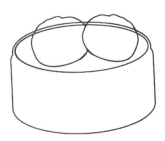

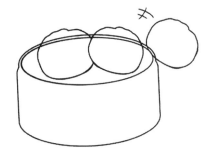

STEP 4   Add a third dumpling slightly outside of the wooden steamer basket. Add two swoosh lines with a third line going across them.

STEP 5

Now, it's time to draw faces! Draw two horizontal lines and a rounded *W*-mouth on the front of the wooden steamer basket. On the first dumpling, draw two dark circle eyes with white highlights and a rounded *W*-mouth. On the middle dumpling, draw one dark circle eye with white highlights, one sideways *V*-shaped eye (to make the dumpling wink!), and a *C*-shaped mouth. On the last dumpling, draw two sideways *V*-shaped eyes and an upside-down *V*-shaped mouth. Add different-length lines to the wooden steamer basket to add depth.

STEP 6

Shade in your drawing and add the finishing touches! Make the inside of the wooden steamer basket the darkest. Create the dumpling folds by darkening sections at the top. Add in small oval blush spots for all of the faces.

DRAWING CHIBI FOOD

Keep going from Step 1.

Try a few from scratch.

MELONPAN

STEP 1 Create an oval with a flatter bottom.

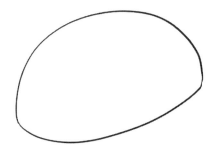

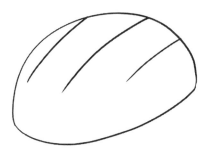

STEP 2 Draw three diagonal lines at the top of the oval shape.

STEP 3 Draw three more diagonal lines at the top of the shape, perpendicular to the previous three lines. Add two circle eyes, two smaller oval blush spots, and a rounded *W*-shaped mouth near the bottom-left side of the oval shape.

STEP 4

Shade in your drawing. Make the melonpan darker at the top and lighter at the bottom. Darken the eyes but leave white spots for highlights.

Keep going from Step 1.

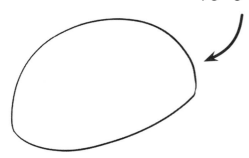

Try a few from scratch.

WESTERN FOOD

PANCAKES

STEP 1 Start with an oval. Add a thin, rounded *U*-shaped line that connects to the oval above it.

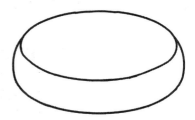

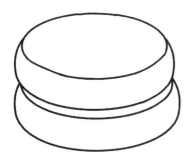

STEP 2 Create a stack by adding another pancake beneath the first. Draw a curved line. Add another thin, rounded *U*-shaped line that connects to the curved line above it.

STEP 3 Add syrup to your pancakes! Starting from the edge of the oval, create syrup drips by drawing squiggles of various lengths. Make a shorter drip near the middle of the drawing to leave space for a cute face!

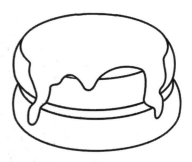

STEP 4

Draw two circle eyes and a rounded *W*-shaped mouth on the front of the top pancake. On the top of the pancake stack, draw a cherry.

STEP 5

Shade in your drawing. Make the cherry, syrup, and top of the pancakes a darker color. Darken the eyes but leave white spots for highlights. Add small oval blush spots.

DRAWING CHIBI FOOD

Keep going from Step 1.

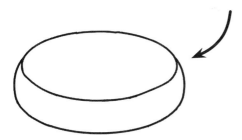

Try a few from scratch.

BACON & EGGS

STEP 1   Draw a circle.

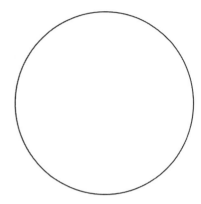

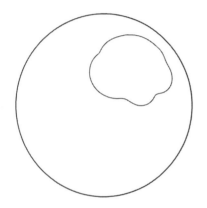

STEP 2   Near the top right of the circle, draw a random blob to represent an egg.

STEP 3   In the bottom left of the circle, draw a piece of bacon by drawing a rectangle with two wavy edges.

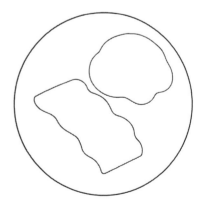

STEP 4

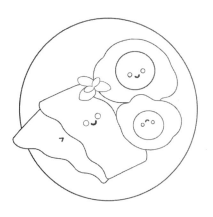

Add another blob underneath the first. Draw two circles within the blobs to create the yolk. Add two small circles and *U*-shaped mouths inside both of the egg yolks. Create another piece of bacon underneath the first by drawing a triangle with a wavy edge that slightly goes over the edge of the circle. Add two circles and a *U*-shaped mouth to the first piece of bacon. Add a sideways *V*-shaped eye to the second piece of bacon. Between the eggs and the bacon, draw a sprig of greens by drawing overlapping ovals.

STEP 5

Add fat to your bacon by drawing parallel wavy lines.

STEP 6

Shade in your drawing. Make the egg yolks darker than the egg whites. Make the bacon fat lighter than the bacon meat. Create a plate border by shading in the middle of the circle.

DRAWING CHIBI FOOD

Keep going from Step 1.

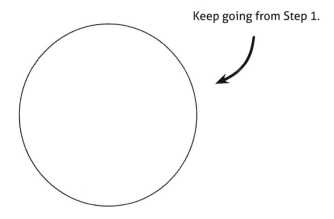

Try a few from scratch.

CROISSANT

STEP 1 Create a lumpy sideways crescent shape for your croissant.

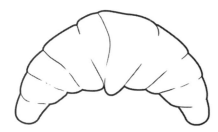

STEP 2 Add curved lines at each lump of the crescent shape.

STEP 3 Add short dark lines in the middle of the crescent shape to add more depth.

STEP 4 Draw a thick swirly line from one side of the crescent to the other (for chocolate).

STEP 5
Create a cute face by drawing two circle eyes, two smaller oval blush spots, and a *U*-shaped smile.

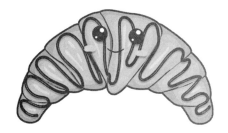

STEP 6
Shade in your drawing. Darken the eyes, but leave white spots for highlights.

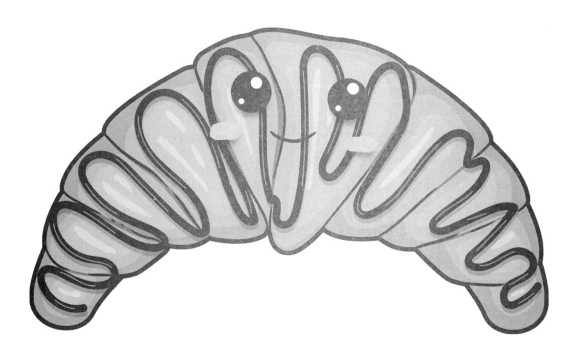

Keep going from Step 1.

Try a few from scratch.

SANDWICH

STEP 1
Draw a rounded triangle shape that is flatter at the top and bottom-right corner.

STEP 2
Create the front piece of bread by drawing two parallel lines from the top corner to the bottom corner (these lines will act as the crust). Make sure to round out the corners and erase the flat line at the bottom-right corner.

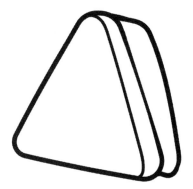

Sketch a few more!

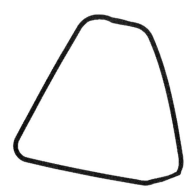

STEP 3
Draw two circle eyes, two smaller oval blush spots, and a small *U*-shaped mouth on the front of the sandwich. On the right of the piece of bread, sketch some thin shapes that connect back to the front piece. Make some round and short (for the tomatoes), some short and pointed (for cheese), and some longer and wavy (for the lettuce). Add some short curved lines throughout the drawing to add more texture.

STEP 4
It's time to shade your sandwich! Darken the eyes but leave white spots for highlights. Make the crust, lettuce, and tomatoes darker than the front piece of bread.

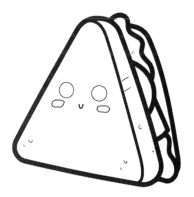

Sketch a few more!

Try a few from scratch.

SPAGHETTI & MEATBALLS

STEP 1 To make a bowl, draw two concentric ovals. Add a curved *U*-shaped line that connects to the bigger oval above it. Erase the bottom left portion of the larger oval to create the rim of the bowl. Add a foot for the bowl by drawing a short thin curve underneath.

STEP 2 Create spaghetti noodles by drawing repeating swirly lines within the bowl.

STEP 3 Add some spaghetti noodles dangling off the rim of the bowl by drawing a few vertical thin curved shapes. At the top of the bowl of spaghetti, add sauce by drawing a shape with a rounded top and a wavy bottom (for sauce drips). Erase any overlapping lines behind the sauce.

STEP 4

Draw two circle eyes, two smaller oval blush spots, and a small *U*-shaped smile. Add three rounded hexagonal shapes for meatballs and two small leaf sprigs on top of the spaghetti and sauce.

STEP 5

Shade in your drawing! Darken the eyes and leave white spots for highlights. Make the sauce darker than the spaghetti noodles and the meatballs darker than the sauce.

Keep going from Step 1.

Try a few from scratch.

TACO

STEP 1 Draw a rounded semicircle with a bump on the right side.

STEP 2 Continue the semicircle and end the line with a slight curve.

STEP 3 Create lettuce by drawing a bumpy curved line around the semicircle.

STEP 4 Add meat to your taco by drawing curved and cloud-like shapes around the lettuce.

WESTERN FOOD

61

STEP 5

Create a cute face by drawing two circle eyes and a small *V*-shaped smile.

STEP 6

Fill your taco with another layer of meat and lettuce. Then add cheese to your taco by drawing small thin rectangles around the meat and lettuce. Shade in your drawing, making the ingredients darker than the taco shell.

Keep going from Step 1.

Try a few from scratch.

PIZZA

Draw a rounded triangle shape with a slight bump at the top-left corner.

STEP 2 Draw a wavy line to make your pizza extra cheesy. Erase where any cheese drips overlap.

STEP 3 It's time to add the crust! Draw a slightly curved line parallel to the top of the pizza slice. This line should start at the bottom of the slight bump at the top-left corner. Sketch a circle in the top-right corner to give your pizza a 3D effect.

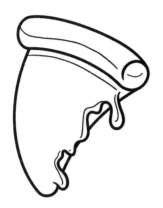

STEP 4

Draw some light lines across your drawing to add more texture.

STEP 5

Sketch some tiny ovals across the drawing. Draw bigger circles for pepperoni.

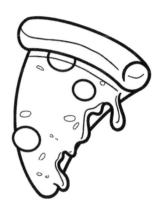

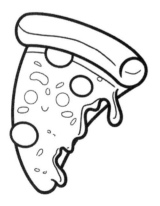

STEP 6

Add two circle eyes, two smaller oval blush spots, and a small *U*-shaped smile. Draw a curved shape above the left eye and a straight shape above the right eye.

STEP 7

Shade in your drawing. Darken the eyes and leave white spots for highlights. Make the crust and pepperoni slices darker than the cheese.

Keep going from Step 1.

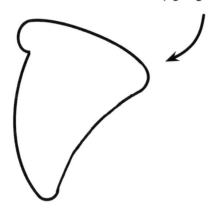

Try a few from scratch.

HAMBURGER

STEP 1
Draw a rounded bun with a flat bottom. Give the bun a thin, squiggly skirt for lettuce.

STEP 2
Add dark eyes with a few white reflection spots and small eyebrows. Underneath the lettuce, sketch some thin, curved shapes that connect to the lettuce above them. Make some rounder and shorter (for the tomatoes or onions) and some longer (for the patties).

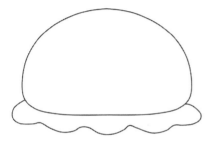

Sketch a few more!

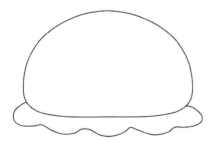

STEP 3

Draw another layer of squiggly lettuce and a rounded bun underneath. Add a cute, *W*-shaped mouth.

STEP 4

Lightly shade the top and bottom buns. Leave some small white spots on top for the sesame seeds and a few spots near the eyes for blush marks. Add darker shades to the lettuce, tomatoes, and patties.

Sketch a few more!

WESTERN FOOD

Try a few from scratch.

FRENCH FRIES

STEP 1 To start the french fry box, draw a rectangular shape with a slightly curved top and right side. Add a thin sideways trapezoid on the right side of the rectangle. At the top, sketch a semicircle and erase any overlapping lines.

STEP 2 Draw pairs of rectangles to create 3D french fries. Make some rectangles short and some rectangles long.

STEP 3 Sketch a thick line (for a right arm). Create a bottle of mustard by drawing a vertical rectangle, a smaller horizontal rectangle, and a thin triangle on top.

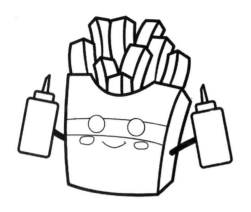

STEP 4

Draw a band across the front of the french fry box and add a cute face by drawing two circle eyes, two smaller oval blush spots, and a *U*-shaped smile. Sketch another thick line (for a left arm). Create a bottle of ketchup by drawing a vertical rectangle, a smaller horizontal rectangle, and a thin triangle on top.

STEP 5

Shade in your drawing. Leave the band a lighter shade than the rest of the box.

WESTERN FOOD

Keep going from Step 1.

Try a few from scratch.

POPCORN

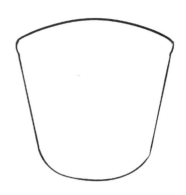

STEP 1 Create a tall rounded trapezoid.

STEP 2 Draw two parallel curved lines to create the opening of the popcorn bucket.

STEP 3 Add vertical lines to the base of the popcorn bucket.

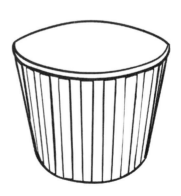

STEP 4 Draw popcorn by sketching a cloud-like shape at the top of the bucket.

STEP 5 Create a cute face by drawing two circle eyes, two smaller oval blush spots, and a rounded *W*-shaped mouth on the front of the bucket. Form individual popcorn kernels by creating a bunch of smaller random blob shapes within the larger cloud-like shape.

STEP 6 Shade in your drawing. Darken the eyes but leave white spots for highlights. Make alternating stripes a darker shade. Lightly shade the popcorn.

Keep going from Step 1.

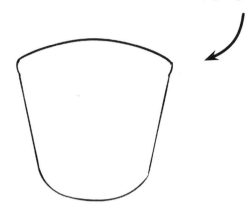

Try a few from scratch.

DRINKS & DESSERT

MILK SHAKE

STEP 1
Start drawing the outline of the milk shake by making a small oval base. At the top of the base, begin the body of the milk shake, getting slightly wider as you go up. At the top, draw the outline of whipped cream.

STEP 2
Define the fluffy whipped cream by drawing curved lines at the top of the milk shake.

STEP 3
Draw five vertical curved lines to make a glass pattern for the milk shake.

STEP 4

Add a cute face by drawing two circle eyes, two smaller blush spots, and a *U*-shaped smile. Draw a cherry on top of the whipped cream by sketching a circle with a thin vertical rectangle for the stem.

STEP 5

Shade in your drawing. Darken the eyes but leave white spots for highlights. Make the milk shake glass and cherry darker than the whipped cream.

Keep going from Step 1.

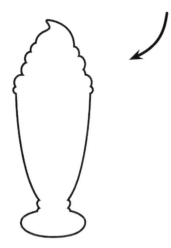

Try a few from scratch.

DRAWING CHIBI FOOD

BOBA

STEP 1 Draw a cup by sketching a tall trapezoid. At the top, draw a thin curved band (for the rim).

STEP 2 Create the lid. Draw a semicircle with a small thin oval at the top. Sketch some additional lines throughout your drawing to add more depth.

STEP 3 Give your cup a transparent 3D effect by adding some curved lines near the rim. Draw a thin rectangular straw. Sketch some additional lines on your straw to add some texture.

STEP 4

Draw three slightly curved lines on the cup. Erase small sections of those three lines to create a 3D effect. Erase where the straw and lid overlap.

STEP 5

Create a cute face by drawing two circle eyes, two smaller oval blush spots, and a tiny *U*-shaped mouth. Add boba by drawing circles of various sizes at the bottom of the cup. Sketch highlight marks on the cup, lid, and straw by drawing ovals.

STEP 6

Shade in your drawing. Darken the eyes but leave white spots for highlights. Make the boba darker than the cup. Add thick white horizontal highlight lines.

DRINKS & DESSERT

Keep going from Step 1.

Try a few from scratch.

MILK CARTON

STEP 1
Draw the outline of a milk carton. It should resemble a thin rectangle on top of a trapezoid on top of a square.

STEP 2
Make the carton 3D. Draw a line to complete the thin rectangle. Separate the trapezoid into a parallelogram and a triangle. Separate the original square into a smaller square and a rectangle.

STEP 3
Draw twelve vertical lines within the thin rectangle. Create two squiggly lines at the base of the carton.

STEP 4 On the bottom right of the carton, draw a shape that resembles two overlapping ovals.

STEP 5 Draw a face on the front of the carton by adding two circle eyes, two smaller oval blush spots, and a sideways curvy *W*-shaped mouth. Add lines to the two overlapping ovals to make them look like a stack of cookies.

STEP 6 Shade in your drawing. Darken the eyes but leave white spots for highlights. Make the top of the carton and the cookies darker than the base of the carton.

Keep going from Step 1.

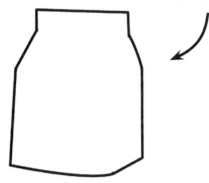

Try a few from scratch.

COFFEE

STEP 1
Start the outline of a coffee cup and saucer with a curved *U*-shaped line. Connect the top points of the *U*-shaped line with a flatter curved line. Add a handle on the right side that resembles a capital *D*. Create a saucer by drawing half of an oval. Erase any overlapping lines.

STEP 2
Create a 3D effect. Draw your coffee cup's opening by sketching a thin pointy oval at the top of the cup. Add two slightly curved lines at the bottom of the *U*-shaped curve to create a foot for the coffee cup. Add a slightly curved line that connects the points of the half-oval saucer.

STEP 3 Add some coffee art! In your coffee cup opening, draw a shape that resembles the top of a heart. Shade that shape in, and erase four concentric curved lines on each side. Also add tiny dots in the opening.

STEP 4 It's time to draw the face! Draw two oval blush spots, two sideways *V*-shaped eyes, two dash mark eyebrows, and a sideways *D*-shaped mouth.

STEP 5 Shade in your drawing. Make the coffee darker than the cup. Add some squiggly lines at the top (for steam).

Keep going from Step 1.

Try a few from scratch.

DRAWING CHIBI FOOD

CUPCAKE

STEP 1

Draw a bowl-like shape that is flat on the bottom, with rounded ridges at the top.

STEP 2

Add an arch that spans across the top of the cupcake wrapper. On the wrapper, draw large, round eyes with a few white spots, and small eyebrows.

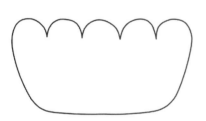

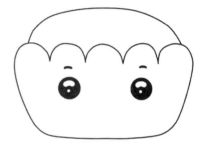

Sketch a few more!

STEP 3

Draw a large swirl of icing, complete with folds and a curl on top. In between and slightly below the eyes, draw a cute, open mouth that starts in the shape of a *W* and extends in a long *U*.

STEP 4

Erase the top line of the cupcake that's covered by the icing. Shade in the cupcake and the icing, leaving lighter spots in the icing for sprinkles. Shade the inside of the mouth, with a lighter shade on the bottom for the tongue. Give your cupcake some adorable blush marks to finish.

Sketch a few more!

Try a few from scratch.

DONUT

STEP 1
Sketch a large, slightly oblong circle. It doesn't have to be perfect!

STEP 2
Draw a thin, pointy oval in the upper middle of the circle to represent the donut hole. Sketch a half-circle over the top of the donut to make the icing. The top of the half-circle should rise just slightly above the top of the donut, while the bottom should have a squiggly edge that ends a little below the center.

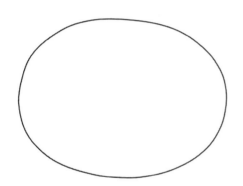

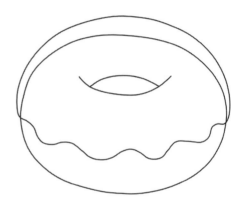

Sketch a few more!

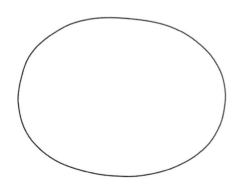

STEP 3
Erase the top line of the donut covered by the icing. Draw eyes with some white reflection spots just below the donut hole. Add a mouth shaped like a rounded *W*.

STEP 4
Shade the icing and donut, making the icing slightly darker. Don't forget to add some white blush marks near the eyes. Color in some fun sprinkles all over the icing.

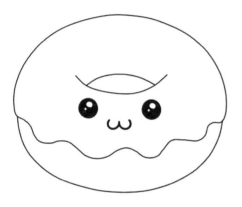

Sketch a few more!

Sketch a few more!

Try a few from scratch.

DRAWING CHIBI FOOD

ICE CREAM CONE

STEP 1
Draw a scoop of ice cream in the shape of a fluffy cloud. Sketch the same pattern of the bottom edge underneath the first scoop.

STEP 2
Add a rectangle coming out of the top right of the ice cream. Draw round, dark eyes with a few white spots, and a *V*-shaped cone.

Sketch a few more!

STEP 3

Erase the line behind the rectangle. Draw a crisscross pattern on the cone. Divide the rectangle on top into six even squares. Draw a simple smile between the eyes.

STEP 4

Make the ice cream scoops different flavors by adding light coloring to the top scoop. Shade the cone and the rectangle and add some blush spots near the eyes.

Sketch a few more!

Sketch a few more!

Try a few from scratch.

CHOCOLATE CHIP COOKIE

STEP 1 Draw a round bumpy shape. Make the top-right portion of the shape a little more rough and jagged.

STEP 2 Add another curved bumpy line near the bottom edge of the shape.

STEP 3 Create small chocolate chips by drawing small round shapes throughout your drawing.

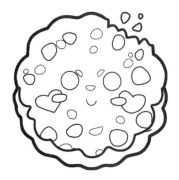

STEP 4 Draw two circle eyes, two smaller oval blush spots, and a *U*-shaped smile. Create bigger chocolate chip shapes. Near the blush spots, make two heart-shaped chocolate chips. At the top right, add small crumb shapes.

STEP 5

Shade in your drawing. Darken the eyes but leave white spots for highlights. Make the chocolate chips a darker shade than the cookie. Shade in the bottom to give your cookie a 3D effect. Add white lines near the chocolate chips as a finishing touch.

Keep going from Step 1.

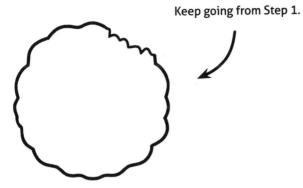

Try a few from scratch.

CAKE

STEP 1 Start the outline of the cake slice by drawing a rectangle with rounded edges. Erase the top line of the rectangle. Draw a diagonal line that starts from the top-left corner of the rectangle. Connect the diagonal line to the top-right corner of the rectangle with four rounded bumps.

STEP 2 Make the cake slice look 3D. Create a layer of frosting by sketching a curved line below the bumps/scallops. Add a vertical line parallel to the right edge of the cake. Draw four horizontal lines of varying lengths to create different cake layers.

STEP 3 Add a strawberry on top! Draw a half-oval shape. Above the half-oval shape draw a trapezoid with a spiked bottom. Add a stem by sketching a thin rectangle.

STEP 4

Draw two circle eyes, two smaller oval blush spots, and a tiny *U*-shaped mouth to the front of the cake slice. Add the finishing details. Draw oval seeds and two diamond highlights within the strawberry. Draw lines to create individual strawberry leaves. Sketch a line that follows the frosting of the cake.

STEP 5

Shade in your drawing. Darken the eyes, leaving white spots for highlights. Make the frosting and strawberry darker. Shade the different cake layers and add three diamond highlights.

Keep going from Step 1.

Try a few from scratch.

MARSHMALLOWS

STEP 1
Draw two round, flat ovals, one inside the other, to form a plate.

STEP 2
On top of the plate, sketch three slightly misshapen circles that overlap and are stacked in the shape of a pyramid.

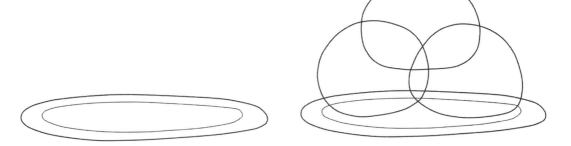

Sketch a few more!

STEP 3

Erase all the lines that are now covered by the two bottom marshmallows so that the top marshmallow appears behind the other two. Give the bottom marshmallows V-shaped hands. For the top marshmallow, add rounded hands resting on top of the lower marshmallows' heads.

STEP 4

Draw cute faces on each marshmallow. Give the puffers lots of character by making each marshmallow different. Draw one with an open-mouthed smile, one with big round eyes, and another with smiling eyes. Finally, make each marshmallow a different shade.

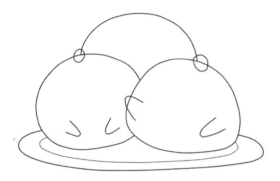

Sketch a few more!

Sketch a few more!

Try a few from scratch.

PRACTICE PAGE

DRAWING CHIBI FOOD

PRACTICE PAGE

Discover More Great How-to-Draw Books from Ulysses Press

Learn more at www.ulyssespress.com